Quest for Meaning

Conversations on the Apostles' Creed

Thomas F. Chilcote

Contents

The Apostles' Creed

I believe in God the Father Almighty, maker of heaven and earth;

And in Jesus Christ his only Son our Lord: who was conceived by the Holy Spirit, born of the Virgin Mary, suffered under Pontius Pilate, was crucified, dead, and buried; the third day he rose from the dead; he ascended into heaven, and sitteth at the right hand of God the Father Almighty; from thence he shall come to judge the quick and the dead.

I believe in the Holy Spirit, the holy catholic Church, the communion of saints, the forgiveness of sins, the resurrection of the body, and the life everlasting. Amen.

Why?—an Introduction

In an era when change is the prevalent mood, even the suggestion that there are some enduring truths is labeled suspect. Those of us who do affirm and try to practice the Christian faith know how often our spirit languishes. We find reason to believe that there persists in almost every human heart a longing for something reliable—not an anchor so much as a gyroscope.

A young businessman committed suicide after fatally shooting his wife and four of his children. A psychiatrist came to the astonishing conclusion: He "is not so different from the rest of us. . . . We would like to believe he is unique . . . but all kinds of unreported violence occurs in families all the time. This instance is only an extreme example of a universal human condition." This fellow, at forty-two, was an enterprising businessman, but his business failed. He lived in an affluent neighborhood, but his house and expensive car became attached to his liabilities. A popular amateur golfer, he spent more time entertaining clients at the country club than in dealing realistically with business affairs at his office. When his pastor got word of the multiple tragedy, he commented that he could not understand it because the children regularly attended Sunday school.

Can a spiritually rootless person survive? Why does each generation ignore so generally the cumulative evidence that spiritual erosion produces human bankruptcy? After more than three decades of ministering to men, women, youth, and children in sickness and grief, in tragedy and heartbreak, in doubt and despair, in loneliness and uncertainty, in futility and frustration, in risk-taking for "kicks" and withdrawal for fear, I am convinced that a recovery of faith—in some instances a *dis*covery of faith —reopens the possibility for meaning and hope.

I find it sensible and exciting to begin with something that combines durability and familiarity. No brief summary of essential Christian affirmations meets such expectations more than the Apostles' Creed. It has ancient rootage, developing out of questions put to candidates for baptism (at least as early as the third century). It gradually was framed into a statement suitable for use in corporate worship or for instruction.

I hope that those who seek new encouragements from this time-honored affirmation will find in the reading of these "Conversations on the Apostles' Creed" heightened joy in their reliance on the goodness and providence of God. I hope that those who may have lost vital touch with the divine—or those who never thought they had it—may sense that the faith which sustained our fathers now offers them nourishment for joyous living.

I have not tried to interpret the phrase "he descended into hell" because this late addition to the Creed does not have universal usage. I also point out that the Creed makes no mention of the Kingdom of God. For Christians in our day this is a matter of great importance. I am mindful of it and rejoice that we are wrestling with its implications and implementation with uncommon earnestness and urgency. The "Sixth Conversation" does have some mention of the church's social thrust as it fulfills its function as the Church Militant.

I owe special thanks to Mrs. Joseph Milam, Jr., secretary of First Broad Street United Methodist Church, Kingsport, Tennessee, for her diligent and careful preparation of the typescript.

—THOMAS F. CHILCOTE

Where We Begin

Scripture Reading: Genesis 1:1-8

Every so often there are those who request a reinterpretation of the Apostles' Creed. There are, of course, those who would like to say that, because of its antiquity dating back some hundreds of years, it ought to be consigned now to the archives and no longer used in public worship.

The use of the Creed in public worship in the twentieth century is hardly intended to serve the purpose of merely perpetuating an ancient statement of faith. Rather, it has won acceptance through the centuries because it is a credo of living affirmations. I am sure other expressions of the Christian faith have been formulated that we no longer use. But there is something about the Apostles' Creed that encourages us to use it as the Body of Christ in our time.

By taking the Creed phrase by phrase, as these conversations attempt to do, we may get a fresh awareness of this remarkable condensation of the Christian faith. Somebody has remarked that the Apostles' Creed is "a truly common expression of early Christendom and can therefore be valid as the confession of our faith." It has also been called "the shortest catechism of Christianity."

We know that by about A.D. 175 the Christians had suffered harshly at the hands of their persecutors. Yet their numbers kept growing, and it became absolutely necessary for them to put into the minds and hearts—if not into the hands—of those who became a part of their fellowship some succinct expression of what Christians were expected to acknowledge. The Creed is called the Apostles' Creed, not because the Apostles had a hand in producing it, but

7

because it was thought to preserve and represent in plain language the teaching of the Early Church which had been under the guidance of the Apostles. Efforts to identify each phrase with one of the Apostles is, therefore, an unsatisfactory and unnecessary exercise because there is no way to confirm such correlation historically.

Armed with this unadorned declaration, Christians defied the pagan world, dignified the life of every man influenced by their faith, and swept their way into history as a people of uncommon splendor.

In this Creed there is no wasted language. All superficiality is stripped away. It possesses a quality of urgency. It is almost fitting to describe it as a briefing for battle, as indeed it was in many of its early uses. It could serve as such a communique in our time as well.

As we undertake these conversations on the Creed, we examine the first living affirmation in this declaration of faith. It begins with two words common to all men: *"I believe."* There is nothing distinctive about that because everyone says, "I believe," either by verbalizing it or acting as though it were verbalized.

The person who says "I do not believe in anything" is most certainly saying "This is what I believe." It is impossible to live as a human being without believing. We may sometimes, wishfully, like to avoid this reality. We may prefer asserting neutrality instead of taking a position. Yet those who assert no faith really assert this neutrality as their faith.

Many years ago a certain boy became an impossible youngster for the police in a Florida city to handle. He was constantly getting into mischief, and his escapades became more and more daring and serious. The police chief heard about a place in Nebraska where this lad might be rehabilitated. So he bought a one-way ticket to Omaha and put the youngster on the train. When the boy was on his way, the chief sent a telegram to Father Flanagan at Boys' Town, describing the young fellow's incorrigibility and instructing Father Flanagan to pick him up at the train station. Father Flanagan accepted the wire's message at face value, not having had any previous contact with the man who sent it. He drove to the station at the anticipated time and, sure enough, found the somewhat bewildered lad.

At Boys' Town, a few miles from Omaha, the school began to work with the new arrival. He was placed in vocational training, but he was not at all interested. He even made some havoc of the woodworking shop. In the dormitory he insisted on making life miserable.

One day Father Flanagan called him into the office. "Why don't you follow the reasonable expectations of those who are trying to teach you?" he asked.

"Nobody can teach me nothin'," came the quick retort.

Father Flanagan, with keen insight, said, "Oh, but you've been going to school all your life."

"No," answered the boy, "I quit school."

"You never quit school," continued Father Flanagan.

"Yes, I did. I lived on the streets and nobody's ever taught me anything."

"Somebody taught you on the streets. Who taught you there?"

The boy began to realize that he could not honestly say, "I have not been taught." Finally Father Flanagan remarked, "You have simply been going to school to the wrong teachers."

Boys' Town recovered that boy. In 1941, in a visit with Father Flanagan, I had this story confirmed. A radiance spread over his face as he told about that young man's eventual accomplishments and new integrity.

So saying "I do not go to school" does not mean "I am not being taught." Nor does saying "I do not believe" mean "I do not have a creed." Everyone says, either positively or negatively, "I believe." There is nothing distinctive about the two words that introduce the Apostles' Creed. They are in the heart, if not on the lips, of every man. Since all men do believe, then it becomes clear that it is *what* we believe that matters.

In what direction do Christians begin to move after they say, "I believe"? They turn to the most natural beginning place: "I believe *in God.*" The Bible could not begin more appropriately than with the affirmation in Genesis 1:1: "In the beginning God." Even though Genesis was not the first portion of scripture produced, it was properly placed first in the canon. In undertaking to tell the story of God's relationship to the world and man, this is where we start. Similarly, a like declaration is a natural beginning point for a Christian creed.

This proclamation of faith in God begins to define the Christian stance in the world. Even when the Creed was first used, belief in God was not a common affirmation. All men may have had belief in some sort or form of deity, but the proclamation of God in the singular and in the absolute quickly reduced the number of persons who would subscribe to the Creed. The Christians did not say, "We believe in gods." They were not polytheists, but they were surrounded by those who did hold such belief. Witness the ancient temples lying in ruin today in Rome, Athens, Byblos, Baalbeck. The Christians did not say "We believe in gods," but "We believe in God."

God in the singular was a peculiarly remarkable development in the evolution of the Hebrew-Christian faith. Even the early Hebrews did not subscribe to the idea of an overarching God in the singular. During their early history in Canaan they believed in a tribal deity. Remember Ruth's words to Naomi: "Your people shall be my people, and your God my God." This clearly reflects a tribal view of deity. But as the centuries passed, the great eighth-century prophets came on the scene to proclaim God in the singular. This carried over into the time of Christ, who himself made firm declaration of God's oneness and his universality.

We can understand the difficulty man experienced in reaching this summit. God is so vast and incomprehensible as to challenge the finite mind. A teen-ager discovered this quotation in Thomas Merton's book, *The New Man:* "He [God] is so far above being that it is in some sense truer to say that he 'is not' rather than 'he is.' Yet, at the same time we best name him who is the fullness of life by saying that 'he is.' And he who 'is' dwells at the heart of our being."

This helps us understand the hesitation men have experienced down through the centuries in affirming God absolutely. He is beyond the finite mind. Relativity has as much bearing on interpreting religion as it has on pursuing scientific investigation. There is more of God than man has been able to affirm. There is more of God than man has yet been able to discover, so there is more of God than man has been able to affirm. There is something more vast than man can comprehend. In a sense we say more about God when we declare he "is not" than when we declare he "is" because we know so little about what he "is." Even so, we know enough to justify affirming his singularity. This is what the Apostles' Creed does at the outset: "I believe in God." Not that we comprehend him in his fullness or apprehend all the truth that resides in his nature, but to the extent we can comprehend the activity of a divine being we affirm God in the universe.

11

Efforts to give credence to this belief have been set forth in many ways. Without enumerating them here, it is worth noting that contemporary efforts to affirm belief in God on the part of scientists and philosophers are largely arrived at in much the same way as the so-called "classical and moral arguments" developed.

The next two phrases are grandly descriptive of God's character and nature: "I believe in God *the Father Almighty, maker of heaven and earth.*" This precise combination of words does not appear in the Bible. These impressions of God are implied in scripture, however. In the Christian revelation, the proclamation of God as Father tempers the proclamation of God as Almighty. There are powers that God possesses which he does not exercise because of his fatherhood. There are some accomplishments of God, functioning as a divine Father, which he would not even attempt as one who had all power.

A child trapped on an upper floor of a burning house was spotted by firemen. They quickly set up a net and called to her to jump to safety. She would not respond. Then a man elbowed through the crowd. He came up to the edge of the net and stretched out his arms. Calling tenderly to the frightened child, using her name, he urged her to jump. She made the leap almost instantly. Someone asked, "Why did she jump for him? He didn't even plead with her." A bystander simply answered, "He is her father." There is a difference of relationship between a child and a fireman and that same child and her father.

Persons who think of God only as Almighty find themselves often alienated from him, even though this limited view may arouse a feeling of awe. When we temper the word *almighty* with the word *Father,* we emphasize warm and ready access into his presence. Our approach comingles respect and love.

12

Something else needs to be said about God as the Almighty: he is a self-limited God. By being self-limited we mean that he voluntarily imposes restrictions on himself. God cannot do certain things because of this self-limitation. If he were to do what he has power to do in all things, he would flagrantly compromise his own character. Some say, for example, that God should act arbitrarily to stop evil in this world. If God were to act in such a way, he would do so at the cost of surrendering his moral nature. This he cannot do. Yet because he is Almighty, the moral law he has designed ultimately has the last word. In that sense he will always be God Almighty.

The phrase "maker of heaven and earth" also reflects distinctive Christian perspective on the marvel of creation. God as the maker of heaven—which is primary in the Creed—means that the earth is placed against the backdrop of something eternal. The earth, being transitory, is set in subordinate relationship to the abiding. Jesus talked about the Kingdom of heaven—interchangeably with the Kingdom of God—not the kingdom of earth or the kingdoms of this world. Indeed, he had little interest in perpetuating a perishable kingdom. This sharply contrasts the view of life prevailing in the time of the early Christians and that pervading the attitudes and outlook of many persons in our time. We affirm that God is maker of heaven and earth, the eternal holding priority over that which is subject to deterioration and ultimate extinction.

These two subtleties of the Apostles' Creed, then, are significant: the word *Father* tempers the word *almighty;* the phrase "maker of heaven" takes precedence over the creation of the earth, putting the changing and changeable in subordinate relationship to the abiding. This logical and exciting perspective is the ground for a reverent as well as a relevant faith.

We may meander in our search for adequate belief in our time, bombarded as we are with a variety of notions. We may indulge in doubt or even toy with revolt, diverting the stream of our lives away from the ultimate. The Pigeon River in the Great Smokies, fed by frequent rains and melting snows, tumbles over the rocks and winds snake-like down its narrow channel. Yet it always flows in the direction of its ultimate—the Gulf of Mexico. However diverse its meanderings, it cannot deny its ultimate end. Life is much like a meandering stream. At birth we begin with no conscious direction at all; and yet, by and by, we can cultivate moral and spiritual sensitivity until we become aware, as did Francis of Assisi, that we are not at peace until we find rest in God.

Prayer

Our heavenly Father, help us to be grateful for the simplification of faith on which we may enlarge as much as we wish but which, when reduced to its essentials, begins with the declaration of trust in you as God in the singular, grateful that you do temper your power with tenderness, and in your wisdom have set that which abides above that which passes away. Amen.

The Near End of God

Scripture Reading: 2 Corinthians 5:18-6:2

We turn now to those words in the Apostles' Creed, *"I believe in . . . Jesus Christ his only Son our Lord."* The Old Testament suggests to us in many ways that God has made persistent overtures to get the attention and arouse the devotion of his highest creation. All these attempts that God made to bring men back into harmony with their divine nature and possibilities, and thus with him, were ultimately eclipsed in the supreme act of God's giving us Jesus Christ.

For us he has become, as someone has described it, "the near end of God." When we read the literature of faith that preceded the coming of Christ into the world, by philosophers as well as by men of religious inclination, we discover that even men of great wisdom found it difficult to comprehend God in the abstract, the distant, the remote. Somehow, when Christ came into the world, men drew closer to God, understanding him better, receiving him more warmly, even obeying him more gladly.

Jesus brought God close. He disclosed God on the level men could comprehend.

What are we proclaiming when we say, "I believe in . . . Jesus Christ"?

When we say "I believe in Jesus," we are not saying so much. This is a common name. It was a common name when it was given to Mary's firstborn son. One of the apocryphal writings, for example, is identified with a man named "Jesus the Son or Sirach." This was long before the time of Christ. The name Jesus was evidently so common that this Jesus was frequently distinguished from the rest, at least when he moved from place to place outside the province of Galilee, as "Jesus of Nazareth." No doubt persons in other places were named Jesus, but he was "Jesus of Nazareth." He had to be identified with the community where he lived most of his life. In our own time there is a professional baseball player whose name is Jesus. Among Spanish-speaking people Jesus is a common name.

We distinguish this Jesus in yet another way—not simply by calling attention to his hometown. We add to his common name a remarkable, descriptive noun: "Christ." We might parallel the need for doing this by calling attention to the fairly common name of the person who serves as the chief executive of the United States, but who is most often referred to as "Mr. President." He is unmistakably identified by his office.

This Jesus of Nazareth is identified best by the use of the designation, Christ. The office or role inferred by this title is that of a person who through his own personality brings God's will to bear uniquely and urgently upon the lives of men. For centuries before Jesus of Nazareth came on the scene, the Jews had the word *messiah* imbedded in their hope. They also used the title "Anointed One" to anticipate the coming of a person who would be set aside by God himself for the special task of effecting reconciliation between man and God. This is a persistent theme in Hebrew scriptures. All of this describes the function of one who would be called Christ. It was a remarkable recognition when Peter said, "You are the Christ!" when Jesus asked the disciples, "Who do you say that I am?"

It is one of the tragedies of history that when Jesus of Nazareth began putting forward the claim that he was Christ and in every imaginable way demonstrated the legitimacy of that assertion, he was rejected by his own people. We all recall that tense moment when he returned to Nazareth after a brief absence. That day in the synagogue he read Isaiah's classic description of the Messiah and his work. After he laid aside the scroll, he turned to the assembly and calmly announced: "Today this scripture has been fulfilled in your hearing." And what happened then? They rose up against him and would have put him to death within the hour by throwing him over a nearby precipice, except that he slipped through the throng and escaped. One of the saddest lines in the New Testament is the observation: "He came unto his own, and his own [those who had long-awaited the fulfillment of the prophecy which he represented] received him not." (John 1:11. KJ) They accepted him as Jesus, but not as Christ.

The overwhelming evidence, both from prophecy and subsequent history (which gives us additional insight), supports the claim Jesus made concerning himself and which he encouraged his disciples to announce as true. When we say we believe in Jesus Christ, we are saying that Jesus of Nazareth fulfilled this holy and distinctive function of acting for God in behalf of alienated men.

The Creed does not proclaim "Jesus teacher," "Jesus prophet," "Jesus example," "Jesus reformer" even though he functioned in all these ways. But any one of these designations would be only partial. The affirmation that Jesus is Christ is far more comprehensive. It embraces all other possible descriptions and much more. His enemies found no difficulty in addressing him, even publicly, as rabbi (teacher) or prophet. Many who have heralded him as the supreme example for man to emulate have yet to accept him as Christ. Those who undertake some humanitarian crusade frequently try to identify Jesus with the desired reform, but they would choose to ignore him if

17

they were expected to call him Christ. Jesus is far beyond Socrates, Jeremiah, Lincoln, Wilberforce—to name only four of the most honored names in history. Jesus excels in attributes and mission any combination of the world's greatest and best. He is the special self-disclosure of God.

Some years ago a book of biographical sketches came on the market. Scores of men and women who contributed richly to the course of civilization were included. Oddly enough, Jesus was left out. Yet, in the lives of many of those whose stories are told, their vast achievements were directly or indirectly attributed to their relationship to Jesus Christ. Instead of using a page or two, whether by accident or design, the compiler did a great service to Jesus by letting him shine through almost every page!

The proclamation that Jesus is Christ, the one sent from God, does not pose any threat to belief in the oneness of God. Saint Paul as a Christian never surrendered his belief in the oneness of God. In writing to Timothy, he vigorously contends: "There is one God and one mediator between God and men, the man Christ Jesus." Paul wrote to the Colossians: "In him the whole fulness of deity dwells bodily." So when we say, "I believe in . . . Jesus Christ," we identify Jesus of Nazareth as the person in the long sweep of history whose life and work brought into full view God's deep longing and desire to woo his wayward children back into joyful relationship with himself. There is no need for another like him to come, nor is there any necessity to expect that God need provide a fuller self-disclosure. The more diligently we let him relate himself to our needs, the more adequate we find him to be.

In my own experience when I sought reconciliation with God, I found Christ excitingly available. Profound ecstasy swept over my spirit as I turned over the lordship of my life from self-control to Christ-control. No one else

18

could have done for me what he did! Since that moment of conscious acceptance of Christ, that experience has grown in validity and value. The passing of many, many years since that memorable night of my encounter has enhanced the joy and warmth that Christ added to my life. In that wonder-filled hour I discovered that Christ did more than inspire me; he possessed me. No one else could have done that for me. Only the one sent from God had the right to make that claim. After it happened I wondered why I had been so reluctant to entrust to him all that was so precious to me. He has done so much more with it than I was doing with it myself!

The Creed adds to its description of Jesus by saying: "Jesus Christ his [God's] only Son." Here we affirm Christ's relationship to God. Again we get help from Saint Paul in understanding Jesus, set forth in 2 Corinthians 5:19: "God was in Christ reconciling the world to himself." The father-son relationship is the closest kind of kinship we know. The New Testament does not hesitate to use the words *Son* and *Father* in describing the close connection between God and Jesus. Emil Brunner put it very well when he said: "God wanted to be wholly understandable to us, and near. Thus he came as man to us. . . . As man, God wanted to come to us men; otherwise he would not really come to us at all. Only a man can we really understand." [1] There is a sufficiency in Jesus Christ as God's only Son.

But the Creed does not stop even there in describing who Jesus is. It goes on to say: "Jesus Christ his only Son our Lord." This adds still another facet to our belief in Jesus. Just as the words "his only Son" affirm what

---

[1] Emil Brunner, *I Believe in the Living God* (Philadelphia: Westminster Press, 1961), pp. 55-56.

Christ is to God, these words "our Lord" signify what Christ wants to be to us.

This was much more critical in the Creed's original historical setting than it may be for us. During the early Christian era the Roman emperors in a long line of succession controlled the empire and every subject by imposing harsh and sometimes vicious demands. Emperor Domitian, to cite one, in A.D. 96 issued a decree setting himself up as deity and demanding, on pain of death, that he be acknowledged by each of his subjects as divine Lord. This meant that Christians had to choose between Domitian and Christ. If they said, "Domitian is Lord," they had no fear of physical harm. But if they said, "Christ is Lord," they risked death by torture. It was that simple and cruel. Many Christians chose Christ—and perished.

Someone may say we are not in such a circumstance in our time. We do not have to reckon with a political tyrant making such a demand of us; but we still must make a choice regarding the lordship of our lives, the control of our lives, the mastery of our lives. It may be that our physical risk is not so great in contrast to that of our spiritual forebears—and even some of our contemporaries —but the subtleties of other masters that are trying to lay hold on or gain control over us, usurping our time, engaging our talents, siphoning off our resources are demands of which we must continually ask: "Are these responses to the lordship of Christ or to some other master?" Every Christian fights this battle. "Who is the Lord of my life?" is a question I must ask myself daily. We should take delight if, in reviewing our lives as Christians, we are able to say, "At every point along the way—in the manner of our speech, in the molding of our attitudes, in the spending of our money, in cultivating our habits, in the choice of our friendships, and what we do for our friends—we have put every expression and action under the lordship and direction of Christ." We should not be the least discouraged or embarrassed when some cynic singles us out for ridicule with some derision like: "Poor fellow, look how much he's missing since he has put his life under Christ's moral discipline and control." We should rejoice that life—our life—can be lived this way!

A recent book that reads like a spiritual classic is *Journal of a Soul.* It consists of the collected writings of John XXIII from his annual retreats across a long span of years. How he gave Christ increasing preeminence! In 1934 he reflected:

When I ask myself what more I can do to please the Lord, and to make myself holy, I find no other answer than this: continue under obedience as you are now; do your ordinary things, day after day, without over-anxiety, without ostentation, but always trying to do them with greater fervour and perfection. . . .

Do not be concerned about your future but think that perhaps you are drawing near the gateway of eternal life. At the same time be ever more content to live like this, hidden from the world, perhaps forgotten by your Superiors, and do not grieve at being little appreciated but try to find an even greater joy in "being esteemed of little worth." [2]

The shining testimony that fairly glistens on every page of this volume is John's deepening devotion to Christ as Lord. When the book is finished, it leaves an entranced reader convinced that under Christ's lordship a life totally committed is not only desirable, but possible.

---

[2] From *Journal of a Soul* by Pope John XXIII. Copyright 1965 by Geoffrey Chapman Ltd. Used with permission of McGraw-Hill Book Company.

Just as Christ enjoys a special relationship to God as his only Son, the Christ surprises us by inviting us to enjoy a special relationship to himself by hailing him as Lord! This is in the confession.

"A person who wraps himself up in Jesus Christ," to paraphrase Emil Brunner, "becomes a new man." If we were to remove everything from human thought and humanitarian service that pertains to or has been inspired by Christ, only then could we begin to appreciate how vast his influence has been. No one else in all history has matched his impact on the minds and hearts of men. It is appropriate that in the Apostles' Creed this affirmation should take such an exalted place: "I believe . . . in Jesus Christ [God's] only Son our Lord."

The Christian makes this affirmation joyfully because he knows how impoverished he would be were it not for Jesus Christ. For us he is "the near end of God."

Prayer

Our heavenly Father, we know that mystery surrounds the magnitude and uniqueness of Jesus Christ, your only Son, our Lord. Yet, for all the mystery and wonder, we feel a warmth in the love and penetration of his spirit into our own hearts. This means that you have accomplished for us what you intended when you sent Christ into the world. May we be joyful as we affirm what we believe about him. May we make more winsome the encouragements we give to others, desiring for them the receiving of Christ for who he is. We offer this our prayer in his wonderful name. Amen.

The Ultimate Desecration

Scripture Reading: Matthew 27:15-26

Now we turn to the next portion of the Creed: *"who was conceived by the Holy Spirit, born of the Virgin Mary, suffered under Pontius Pilate, was crucified, dead, and buried."*

These phrases are separated by commas and become a unit within the Creed. This is all that the Creed has to say about the earthly life of Jesus. Here we recite a brief and plain proclamation of what we might describe as the ultimate desecration. It is a frightful and terrible thing when a bad man works havoc on a good man. This desecration involving Jesus is more distressing than that. It tells us about men who thought themselves good, seeking to destroy the God-man.

The phrases, "conceived by the Holy Spirit, born of the Virgin Mary," were not included in the Creed to incite men to debate the divinity-humanity of Jesus. Unfortunately, many have done this. We have here a simple declaration that in Jesus Christ were combined, as in no one else, the divine and the human. This was the simplest way to say it. The phrasing is both reverent and specific. It was necessary to include it in the Creed because men of that day tried, even as men now try, to prove or disprove one side or the other of the dual nature of Jesus. Some were saying he was totally divine; others insisted he was totally human. The Apostles' Creed simply affirms that he was the God-man, perfectly joining together the divine and the human. So they put it together in the phrases, "conceived by the Holy Spirit [to emphasize his manifest divinity],

23

born of the Virgin Mary [to affirm his real humanity]."
They were saying that, as far as Christ is concerned, he
defied all our common categories for explaining him.

Thomas Dekker, a relatively obscure dramatist of the
seventeenth century, said of Jesus:

> ... the best of men
> That e'er wore earth about him was a sufferer;
> A soft, meek, patient, humble, tranquil spirit,
> The first true gentleman that ever breathed.

Those who take upon themselves his garments and his
spirit become the true gentlefolk of their age.

Men are not only inclined to debate the nature of Jesus.
They have dealt more harshly with him than with anyone
else who has appeared on the human scene. Listen to what
the Creed says next: "suffered under Pontius Pilate, was
crucified, dead, and buried."

When I was fifteen years old, a traveling group of
players came to the city where I was living to present a
version of "The Passion Play." They engaged a large
stage in the city. I was eager, even as a young teen-ager,
to witness this dramatization of the portentous final events
in the life of Jesus. So I went to see the play. It was a
gripping story. As much as I had heard about Jesus in
Sunday school and in sermons, it had never really regis-
tered with me what abuses men had imposed upon him
until I saw "The Passion Play." I was so startled and
affected by it that I went back the next night, and the
next. It became more compelling each time I viewed it.
Even though the presentation required about three hours
and the only seat I could afford was high up in the balcony,
I was as rapt in my interest the third time as I was the
first night I saw it.

Years later, when I traveled to Oberammergau to see the classical version of the play, the time required for presentation—almost eight hours—sped swiftly. In that setting I did not understand the language, and I did not attempt to follow with great care the English translation in the program as the tableaux and scenes unfolded, but I fully comprehended what was taking place. Here is the one *event* known almost universally. Even the non-Christian world can hinder it only for a little while!

Something is vastly more important, however, than seeing this enactment on the stage, no matter how splendid the staging may be. Such drama serves only to reinforce in our minds that the torment Jesus experienced is more poignant and profound than might be caught up in the anguished cry, "man's inhumanity to man." Could it be that all the elements contributing to this event conspired to be *man's inhumanity to God?*

As I ponder the episodes that constitute the Passion of our Lord and continue reading the Gospel narratives, I see more and more vividly that what happened to Christ during his brief humanity is that he was the victim of man's iniquity at its flood. Men deliberately desecrated the holy, deliberately tried to drive off and out of their immediate presence this supreme expression of the nearness of God. Men seem to be exceedingly uncomfortable with God close up. So frightful is our alienation from our heavenly Father and so insidious our irreverence that we have little compunction of conscience when it comes to devastating whatever is pure.

The havoc wrought upon Jesus Christ makes it appear that evil looks upon it as a great boon when persons in whom purity and goodness are embodied are subjected to shameful treatment, even put to death. Does it not deeply disturb us that the death of Jesus was demanded by men who sincerely laid claim to righteous living and yet could not tolerate the closeness of God? Who, apart from Jesus Christ, has ever made purity so evident and truth so clear? At his self-achieved best, man cannot comfortably draw near to Christ.

Notice now that the Creed does not say, "condemned by Pontius Pilate." Jesus was not condemned, even by the Roman governor who gave consent to the crucifixion! Pilate declared Jesus innocent. Nor does the Creed say, "convicted by Pontius Pilate." He was not convicted by him. He was declared good by Pilate.

Notice, too, that the Creed makes no mention of the initiative taken by the leaders of the Jews to have Jesus crucified. This may have been omitted for two reasons. First, the Christian wanted the Jews to acknowledge Jesus as Christ and thus open up the door for their restoration to God; second, and more important than that, the early believers were wise enough to know that cosmic guilt put Jesus on the cross. It was not a national guilt, not the demand made by a few, but the act of all mankind.

Even though Jesus won clear acquittal before the tribunal of the Empire when Rome's representative publicly proclaimed the guiltlessness of Jesus, yet it is true that he "suffered under Pontius Pilate." Nor was Jesus insensitive to the ordeal. One of my teachers in New Testament said concerning these cruelties approved by Pilate and Herod that Jesus' divinity did not diminish but increased his pain. He was not only aware of the tortures inflicted upon his body, but he was sensitive to what men were doing to their own souls as they sadistically put him through psychological as well as physical torment.

Peculiar ugliness and awfulness accompany death by crucifixion. We speak of the cross almost unemotionally and wear it gratefully as a symbol of our faith. We hardly

26

comprehend that it took three centuries before the Christians would even accept the cross to represent their devotion to Christ, so much did they despise it.

In the case of Jesus, the crucifixion was the more shameful because the preliminary abuses were bald caricatures. The ignominies to which he was subjected before he was impaled on the cross are alluded to, but not set forth in elaborate detail in the Gospel narratives. Some say, "He must have been a weakling to have fallen under the cross on the way to Calvary. Look at the other two who climbed the hill that morning with him to be crucified. They evidently made it all the way without assistance." The record reminds us that Jesus had no nourishment for at least twelve hours. He was scourged by the soldiers. Dr. Edwin McNeil Poteat, in describing this action, believed thirty-nine lashes were laid across Jesus' back, a torture under which many victims frequently died. He was subjected to merciless mockery, spat upon, blindfolded, slapped on the face, scorned, crowned with thorns.

The crucifixion itself was carried out under the gaze of as international a group of spectators as could have been assembled in the first century. This is attested by the use of three languages in the inscription nailed to the upright over Jesus' head.

What did all this accomplish? While it seemed to be serving the purposes of his enemies, it turned out that Christ's suffering, crucifixion, death, and burial brought God himself into the very center of our human predicament. The apostle Paul, recalling this infamous day, spoke a lasting truth when he sent this word off to his friends in Philippi: Christ "emptied himself. . . . And being found in human form he humbled himself and became obedient unto death, even death on a cross." God was in the center of it, bringing final good out of it.

Christ is not our companion in our sinning, but he did not shrink from the ordeal sinful men devised and imposed on him. We compelled him to experience the carnality of our arrogant separation from God. Our spiritual disobedience and alienation enabled us to take uncommon pleasure in working havoc on his exemplary life. It is a thought to ponder that we took the best brother the human race has ever known and did all this to him.

Who among us would dare say that if Christ were among us now we would resist sinful men and champion him? The depth of our guilt and the profundity of our alienation from God still haunt us when exalting Christ becomes a prime issue.

The crucifixion is not just something a few men did to a good man. In the upper room, before the crucial events began, the disciples felt that any one of them might have it within their temperament to betray him. Remembering that, it would be difficult for anyone else to take a superior attitude, saying we would engage ourselves in his defense.

Even the best among us is tempted to withdraw from considering himself a party to Jesus' crucifixion. It is more to our liking to look at this event objectively as a bad hour in history. We talk about it quite unemotionally and casually. We avoid participating in the Sacrament of the Lord's Supper, using some of the poorest excuses; and yet this very act in which we can engage is intended to keep the fact of Jesus' death upon the cross vividly in our remembrance. He said this was what it was to signify!

The cross was a crisis in God's dealing with men. We know that if Christ's suffering and death accomplished anything at all in revealing God's redemptive love at work, then we must consider this event, not as objective history only, but as subjective experience. We must let it open up for each of us a confrontation between ourselves and God.

Notwithstanding the horror of these cruelties imposed on our Lord, there is something magnetic about them. If on a visit to Jerusalem one seeks out the place that might have been the Calvary on which Christ died, he is directed to a spot that does not seem to be a conspicuous hilltop. It is rocky, barren, rugged. In more recent centuries it has been used for burials, with various kinds of sarcophagi placed on its knoll. There it is; its exposure to the sun makes the midday unbearably hot. You stand back from it, contemplate its meaning, and carry away an indelible memory of it. That bleak hilltop seems to be bathed in gloom even on the sunniest afternoon. This event, with all the kindred places that remind us of it, forever attracts us. We cannot take our eyes off it. The whole panorama of the deed against Christ is austere, and so is the language of the Creed that tells us about it: He "was crucified, dead, and buried."

Does this portion of the Creed have the power to stir our hearts? Does it have any influence in compelling us to examine more carefully our own spirit? Through the ages men who have grieved over this gross dealing with Christ have been drawn closer to God—and when this happens to even one of us, all the suffering was worth it. Hebrews 12:2 carries that almost incomprehensible sentence concerning Jesus, ". . . who for the joy that was set before him endured the cross, despising the shame." He did not expect or call for deliverance from suffering. He hoped instead that men would gaze upon him and then pray: "If God will go as far as this to prove his love for us, we will give him our hearts in full devotion." When this happens in the life of any person, whoever he or she may be, then what Christ endured takes on the victory that gave him joy.

The problem is with us. We want blessing without discipline; redemption without repentance; peace without confession of guilt; happiness without spiritual refinement. We want all the good things of life free. We look at our weaknesses. We recognize our rebelliousness against God in so many ways—even after saying we accept Christ! We find it hard in day-by-day encounters to keep bright in spirit and warm of heart. The tug on us by our age, given over so totally to secularism and materialism, reminds us again and again that it is not hard for a mob to persuade even the innocent to cry out, "Crucify him, crucify him!"

When we think we have discharged our relationship to the cross by recognizing it as an agonizing event in history, never really taking its deeper implications to heart, then it is little more than a jest of fate. The time has long since gone, if indeed it ever was, when men could indulge in the luxury of debating and arguing about Jesus—either who he was or what he did. We need to affirm and proclaim him as the one he claimed to be. Only then can we enter into a truly satisfying relationship with him.

When Jesus came to Golgotha they hanged Him on a tree,
They drave great nails through hands and feet, and made a Calvary;
They crowned Him with a crown of thorns, red were His wounds and deep,
For those were crude and cruel days, the human flesh was cheap.

When Jesus came to Birmingham, they simply passed Him by,
They never hurt a hair of Him, they only let Him die;
For men had grown more tender, and they would not give Him pain,
They only just passed down the street, and left Him in the rain.

Still Jesus cried, "Forgive them, for they know not what they do,"

30

And still it rained the winter rain that drenched Him through
  and through;
The crowds went home and left the streets without a soul to
  see,
And Jesus crouched against a wall and cried for Calvary.

These are familiar lines, but is the title G. A. Studdert-
Kennedy gave that poem familiar? He called it "Indiffer-
ence." We can take the same attitude toward this portion of
the Apostles' Creed, or we can let it lead us to admitting
our involvement in the guilt that assaults purity and truth.
More wonderfully, we can let it lead us beyond confession
to accepting the redemption it promises.

Our hour to affirm him is now—in this particular moment while our generation enjoys its brief sojourn on this
planet. We have no other time!

So here the words are once more: "I believe . . . in Jesus
Christ . . . who was conceived by the Holy Spirit, born of
the Virgin Mary [the God-man], suffered under Pontius
Pilate [not convicted or condemned, but suffered], was
crucified [a dark hour for God and man], dead [confirmed
by every certainty], and buried." Imagine saying this about
the best that God ever gave!

Prayer

Our Father, may these words that we sometimes recite
so easily become for us testimony and not merely familiar
repetition. In such a plain and concise proclamation of
Jesus Christ and what he did, may we see a renewed invitation to give ourselves to you in deeper gratitude for
your Son's having given himself for us. Amen.

31

Fourth Conversation

The Triumph of Righteousness

Scripture Reading: John 20:19-29

As we begin this fourth conversation on the Apostles' Creed, we need to remember again that this formulation was probably used by the Early Church as a brief catechism for new Christians. It was designed to give them some understanding of what the Christian faith should signify to them. Without easy access to the scriptures, the Christian found the Apostles' Creed exceedingly helpful as a quickly understood commentary of the gospel.

We also ought to think of it as a militant kind of battle-cry used by the early Christians to give them courage and to provide mutual strength as they lived out their new faith in a suspicious and hostile environment.

We are glad the Creed does not end with the words, "crucified, dead, and buried." It goes on to say, *"the third day he rose from the dead; he ascended into heaven, and sitteth at the right hand of God the Father Almighty; from thence he shall come to judge the quick and the dead."*

Every one of these declarations has biblical warrant and origin. For example, the resurrection on the third day is recorded in Matthew 28:2-15; Mark 16:1-11; Luke 24:1-12; and John 20:1-18. Christ's ascension is described in Mark 16:19; Luke 24:50-51; Acts 1:9. His sitting at the right hand of God is set forth in Mark 16:19, and his role of ultimate judge is declared in such passages as 1 Corinthians 4:4-5 and 2 Timothy 4:1 and 8.

Since these affirmations were derived from the testimony and eyewitness accounts of those who were closely associated with Jesus and the events following his crucifixion, we can accept them with full confidence. If we give credence to other contemporary testimony concerning secular events, why should we hesitate to receive the testimony that comes to us concerning Christ from those who were willing to risk their lives to declare what they saw and heard about him?

Most of us are better acquainted with the resurrection story than with the accounts of the ascension or with the scriptural interpretations of Christ's role in the final judgment of each person's life. In all these areas of his work following his earthly ministry, there are significant truths that need not be neglected, nor should they be. Here, then, we shall consider them.

We turn first to the phrase, "the third day he rose from the dead." Thomas Jefferson is held in high esteem because he made such a rich contribution to the American style of government. When he ventured into the realm of interpreting the Christian faith, however, he subscribed only to what he defined as "The Life and Morals of Jesus." For that reason he felt inclined to extract from the Gospel record of Christ's life and work a purely reasoned view that removed all the supernatural elements. The copy I have of Jefferson's little book in my library is more of a curiosity than a book of reference. It lacks the inspiration and excitement of the Gospels because it totally lacks the element of marvel. He ends up accepting Jesus only as a teacher, a good man. He accords him no other significance. Interestingly enough, his "reasoned" gospel ends with the bleak sentence: "There laid they Jesus, and rolled a great stone to the door of the sepulchre, and departed."

We are involved with the supernatural when we talk about this portion of the Creed. But whoever eliminates it takes away the glory of the faith that Christ inspires.

The resurrection for the first Christians, and for us

today, is the most important element in our faith. The longer we live the more important and exciting does our affirming of the resurrection become. What we are saying when we recite, "on the third day he rose from the dead," is this: "The grave is not the end. Thanks be to God!"

Joseph Fort Newton's autobiography includes a recollection from his childhood. This is how he described in *River of Years* an unforgettable experience that profoundly affected his spiritual outlook:

A hush fell over our home. Father was very ill. Once, slyly, I got a glimpse of him—his head turning to and fro in agony. The next time I saw him he was white and still and untroubled; he was among the silent people we call the dead. On a snowy day when a keen wind was blowing—a "norther," we called it—my father was buried; a wood fire was burning nearby. Clinging to the hand of my little mother, I looked for the first time into an open grave—to a sensitive child a strange, terrifying experience.

The old country minister adjusted his glasses and read the words of Jesus, "I am the resurrection and the life—Let not your hearts be troubled." Never shall I forget the power of those words. It was as if a great, gentle Hand, stronger than the hand of man and more tender than the hand of any woman, had been put forth from the Unseen to caress and heal my spirit—from that day to this I have loved Jesus beyond the power of words to tell! . . . Forty-six years later I stood on the same spot, when my little mother was laid away; and again the words of Jesus—calm, unhurried, confident—spoke to me out of the depths of death—nay, out of the heart of God—and there was sunrise in the west! [3]

Whoever omits the resurrection from the gospel leaves

---

[3] From the book *River of Years* by Joseph Fort Newton. Copyright, 1946, by Joseph Fort Newton. Reprinted by permission of J. B. Lippincott Company.

out the victory, for it is a triumph of righteousness. The enemies of Jesus were quite sure at the end of Good Friday that the placing of the body in the sepulchre was their last reckoning with him. They said, as it had always been said of other men, destroy his body and you destroy his life. Put him in the tomb and you silence him forever. It was as final an act as men could devise. But this was not the last word spoken concerning Jesus. It was not for men to speak that word. It was for God to utter.

Support for believing in the resurrection is the integrity of the disciples who saw him alive, close-up, and willingly accepted martyrdom because they believed it. The Gospel record of their involvement in these events is full of holy excitement, moving freely from the living Lord's participating in a meal to his appearing in a room even though the doors were shut. His presence, however he manifested himself on the many occasions described in the record, was not fantasy.

The disciples were convinced. They believed from that time on that death would not be any more final for them than it was for him. Just as significant is the testimony of the men whose evil designs were thwarted by this incredible reversal. They set to work at once to discount it, frantically making every imaginable effort to distort the report. They even bribed the soldiers who were in the garden at the time to get them to misrepresent what they had witnessed at the sepulchre. (Matt. 28:11-15) So whether we take the word of Jesus' friends or enemies, we come out with the same conclusion: "the third day he rose from the dead." When we proclaim this we affirm, as did the early Christains, that the grave is not the end.

What are we saying when we declare: "he ascended into heaven, and sitteth on the right hand of God the Father Almighty"? Here we are saying, in effect, "This world

35

is not all." The ascension, like the resurrection, was for Jesus' disciples both a physical and a spiritual event. The mystery is not explainable, but for them and so for us the reality is significantly attested by men of veracity.

Jesus himself loved the world, but he was not enamored of it. He did not want to leave it any more than anybody else in the prime of life does. His agony in the Garden of Gethsemane was genuine. But neither did he become so attached to the world that he could not let it go. Nor did he become so absorbed in it as to forget the Kingdom that overarches and outlasts it. He encouraged his friends not to become charmed by this present world. He said to them, "Do not lay up for yourselves treasures on earth, where moth and rust corrupt and where thieves break through and steal, but lay up for yourselves treasures in heaven. . . . For where your treasure is, there will your heart be also." (Matthew 6:19-21) As for himself, he was committed to the abiding Kingdom. At his trial he allayed the anxiety of Pilate, who feared Jesus might be his or even the emperor's rival. The Master told this puppet of Caesar's: "My kingdom is not of this world." (John 18:36.KJ) Jesus lived gratefully on the earth, but his primary identity was with the Kingdom eternal.

This is a higher citizenship most of us have difficulty accepting. We would like to think we have a corner on this present world. We assume that one of the primary responsibilities we must discharge is making sure we garner to ourselves as much of this world's goods as possible. This, we honestly believe, will guarantee security. So we get caught up in a frantic, sometimes exhausting, effort.

I am glad I was part of a family in which this present world and its goods did not mean very much. Enough to provide a nourishing table, adequate clothing, comfortable shelter, and encouragement to prepare for a useful life—

this was it. My father felt peculiar joy and excitement as he sang the old song which his children also came to cherish:

> I am a stranger here, within a foreign land
> My home is far away upon a golden strand;
> Ambassador to be from realms beyond the sea,
> I'm here on business for my King.

That was all that mattered, and he managed to pass on this perspective to his family. He helped us detach ourselves in large measure from this present world. He never encouraged us to desire the accumulation of material wealth. He gave us instead a deep longing to establish our citizenship in the Kingdom that lasts forever.

Added to the phrase "he ascended into heaven" is the announcement, "and sitteth at the right hand of God the Father Almighty." Reentering the Kingdom eternal after undertaking a divine mission among men on earth, to the complete satisfaction of God the Father, Christ was given his special place of close, continuing identity with God. He had been faithful to the obligation given him. He sits at the right hand of God the Father in testimony to the faithfulness with which he accomplished his earthly purpose. What a fitting consummation for such a difficult mission!

Let us be grateful that the one we call the Lord of our lives is the one who demonstrated and believed that this world is not all there is.

Finally, "from thence he shall come to judge the quick and the dead." Just as the resurrection scoffs at the grave as the end of our being, just as Christ's ascension dramatically demonstrated that this present world is not all, this phrase from the Creed tells us that human judgment is not final.

Roman jurisprudence prided itself in its humane administration of justice. From our vantage-point in history, we look upon the imposition of Roman law as a system that thrived on cruelty and threat, backed up by military might. You will recall that this was the system that took Jesus, an innocent man, and made him a victim of public scorn and torture. But human judgment is not final. There is a higher law to be adjudicated when all the courts of men have fulfilled their function. The moral law, which is God's handiwork, supersedes all the other laws by which men are governed. The imposition of the moral law as the law by which all are to be ultimately judged is God's responsibility. It is fitting that the administering of this law is in the hands of him who experienced the human predicament and who himself suffered under the judgments of men.

Some there are who hold the notion that God's final mercy gives them the liberty of indulging in any kind of living they please here on earth. Their inevitable transition into the Kingdom eternal will be a blessed transition, they assume, because a God of love would not do them harm. Such a stance finds no justification in scripture or even in plain logic. It is folly to indulge ourselves as we jolly well please with the expectation that God's kindness will cancel out our disobedience. Persons who exploit their own lives or the lives of others are held morally responsible and accountable by God. Even though they may escape the judgment of men, they are under the more critical indictment of the moral law. Ultimately each life is judged by Christ. The realism of judgment, someone has pointed out, is caught up in three precise phrases: "He *shall* come to judge; He *has* come; He *comes*." The Christian faith insists that no man is really without intimation of what to expect, whether his life is good or evil.

The universal application of the moral law is implied by the words, "the quick and the dead." No man comes off untouched. All men come under judgment. This is not to say that we should fear it. Most of us can walk into any court in the land and experience no distress because we have done nothing amiss. No indictment has been made, so no penalty will be imposed. With the acceptance of Christ as Lord we can so live under his command and control that, when we finally come before his presence to be judged, we will have nothing to fear. It will be Christ's own testimony that, having won consent to order our lives by his Spirit, we are not under the indictment of the moral law.

How joyous it is to live with an awareness of Christ's presence, discovering that he offers us redemptive guidance with the hope of testifying in our favor because we have let our lives serve as instruments for fulfilling his unfinished work among men! Whatever judgment men may make of a man, so often subjecting goodness to persecution, the judgment of Christ is all that finally counts.

So this portion of the Apostles' Creed encourages us— in fact, compels us—to give serious consideration to final things. We do not live as if the grave were the end because Christ's victory over death demonstrated this is not so; we do not live as if this world were everything to us, but frankly acknowledge that this world is not all there is; we spend our time on earth under a lordship that makes it a joy to affirm that human judgment is not final and that the judgment of God, which is final because it is based on the moral law, promises to open up to us a lasting relationship with him.

So the Creed magnifies these living affirmations: "the third day he rose from the dead" (the grave is not the end); "he ascended into heaven, and sitteth at the right hand of God the Father Almighty" (this world is not all) ; "from thence he shall come to judge the quick and the dead" (human judgment is not final).

As we consider these words of the Creed, we are led to face up to the crucial question: Am I giving due consideration to final things?

Prayer

Our heavenly Father, sometimes we know that William Wordsworth expressed our feelings all too well when he wrote:

> The world is too much with us: late and soon,
> Getting and spending, we lay waste our powers:
> . . . .
> We have given our hearts away, a sordid boon!

Then we come again upon the majestic affirmations of the Apostles' Creed. A new light breaks in upon our minds, and we feel the stirring of your Spirit that calls us to labor more earnestly in anticipating final things. Enable us, O God, to claim Christ's lordship so that victory over the grave, citizenship in the Kingdom eternal, and innocence under moral judgment will ultimately give us the victory. In the name of him who in triumph has gone before us, we pray. Amen.

The Indwelling God

Scripture Reading: John 16:1-11

We come now to a very short phrase in the Creed: *"I believe in the Holy Spirit."*

Many books have been written about the Holy Spirit. I am sure you have read some of them. There is a great deal of biblical material about the work of the Holy Spirit. For example, the power of the Holy Spirit is promised to the disciples in Luke 24:49 and Acts 1:8; the witness of the Spirit is emphasized in Acts 5:32 and Ephesians 1:13-14; the fruit of the Spirit is listed in Galatians 5:22. Because this theme has such vast range in biblical reference, I am going to limit this conversation to that scripture that sets forth Jesus' presentation of the Holy Spirit as he shared with his disciples on the last night he spent with them before his crucifixion. You find this record in John 16.

When we say, "I believe in the Holy Spirit," we subscribe to the belief that God makes his influence pervasive in the world and that he also makes it personal for those who will receive it. It is natural that Jesus would have drawn himself into close human fellowship with the disciples. It follows just as naturally that when he began to talk to them about being taken away from them by crucifixion they began to be sorrowful. Yet he transformed that moment of deep sadness into one of great expectation by saying, "If I do not go away, the Counselor will not come to you."

The word *counselor* needs some interpretation. It was a quite precise word, combining two words from the Greek language. Together, these words mean "one called to the side of another." What Jesus was saying to the disciples was this: "When I go away I will send one whom I am calling to be at your side." So the word is translated "Counselor." In some other translations the English rendering is "Comforter." It really signifies that after Jesus was taken from the disciples' immediate presence, God would not leave them without some manifestation of himself.

It was to their advantage, Jesus said, that he should go away and that the Holy Spirit should come to them. We might ask, "What advantage could possibly come of that?"

The answer would be that so long as Jesus was with them they had to stay in his physical presence in order to get the full benefit of his help. Now the time was near for proclaiming the redemptive love of God in other places. These men would have to be dispersed, separated from each other, to fulfill their particular assignments. Jesus could not go with each one. It was to their advantage that Christ be taken from them as a physically present being and that the Holy Spirit should come into them as an indwelling power. Then, even though they would be scattered, as indeed they were within a very short time after that night, they would not be forlorn. Only by the presence of the Holy Spirit would they have continuing encouragement, understanding, and fortitude to withstand all that would assail them.

These were not melodramatic or idle words that Jesus spoke to his friends. They would indeed be brought before tribunals, and most of them would in time be put to death for his sake. Of that little company of men, according to traditions—except for the scriptural account of the death of James the son of Zebedee in Acts 12:2—all but one died as martyrs; and almost all of them in remote places. Who was with them when they bore their testimony for their Lord in India, Africa, Achaia? Who was with them? Was it Christ in the flesh? No! Was it Christ in vision or apparition? No! It was the Holy Spirit in their hearts.

The coming of the Holy Spirit as announced by Jesus guarantees uninterrupted fellowship between those who love God and God himself, no matter where they may be.

Turn now to what Jesus had to say about the relationship of the Holy Spirit to the world, to individuals who acknowledge Jesus, and to Christ himself. This very simple outline, drawn from very plain scripture, we shall now develop a little.

First, look at what Jesus said would be the relationship of the Holy Spirit to the world. He said: "When he comes [into the world after I have left it], he will convince the world of sin and righteousness and of judgment." (John 16:8) He was saying that the activity of God as carried out by the Holy Spirit would prick the consciences of men who by choice were outside God's love. He would take those who were in spiritual rebellion and show them how self-destructive their rebelliousness was. He would take men who were deliberately pursuing selfish goals, ignoring the pleading of God, and reveal to them their foolhardiness and the futility of their pursuits.

The late Dr. Sam Shoemaker wrote about the Holy Spirit in his book, *With the Holy Spirit and with Fire:* "I think of Him as the roving Center of all God's activity in the world." If the Holy Spirit did not function in this way in behalf of the wayward, there would hardly be any chance to persuade them of God's pursuing love and of his wooing of their hearts. It really says that God is not alienating himself from his rebellious children, but he makes constant, continuous overtures to all his children whether they respond or not.

In the second place, Jesus had something to say about the relationship of the Holy Spirit to those who make an acknowledgment of Jesus as Christ. He said to his friends in the upper room that night: "When the Holy Spirit comes [into your life], he will guide you into all the truth."

We know that revelation is progressive. This is true of the most elementary effort we put forth to try to understand meanings. We see it in the classroom. Parents would be troubled if they had a third grader of whom it was expected he should comprehend trigonometry. They are quite satisfied that their children begin with a mastery of simple numbers, then some uncomplicated combinations, and finally tackle more complicated formulae. So we begin with simple things and gradually venture into the more intricate.

The same procedure applies to God's disclosure of his will and character to our questing minds. It was fitting that Jesus said, in announcing the coming of the Holy Spirit: "He will lead you [not, he will make a sudden, miraculous disclosure] into all the truth." (John 16:13. Moffatt)

The word *all* is important in this sentence because it properly reminds us that truth wherever we find it in whatever category is God's truth. We sometimes get the idea that the Holy Spirit opens up to us only theologically oriented issues. This is not true. Truth is significant to God and for us in all realms. If the Church in the Middle Ages had respected this one little word in this one brief verse of scripture (John 16:13), it would have saved itself the indignity of battling the birth of the modern scientific era, made unpleasantly dramatic by such acts as banning the writings of Copernicus and the unjustified harassment of Galileo. If the Church of that age had lifted up this assertion of Jesus that the Holy Spirit leads us into *all* the truth, the ecclesiastics would have been less intent on limiting the areas in which they considered the Holy Spirit to be active.

Of more recent vintage is the ridiculous sophistry that took place in the courthouse at Dayton, Tennessee, on the topic of evolution—another fiasco that would never have occurred had the principals in the case been more sensitive to the little word *all* in John 16:13.

When anyone lays hold on an objective fact of history, this is a discovery he makes through the functioning of the Holy Spirit in his mind. A fact of history is a fragment of truth worth knowing, so it is brought by the Holy Spirit to the inquirer's attention.

This principle also keeps us from assuming that the only important revelations of God are accomplished by miracle —the setting aside of the normal operation of natural law. I recall a story my father shared with us, his children, as we, one by one, left home for college. He expected us to be faithful to our studies and make disciplined use of our time. He had an experience in college which he thought might help us. On a particular day a Greek examination was scheduled. His roommate and he were in the same class. Early in the evening before the examination, his roommate got down beside his bed and prayed something like this: "Now, Lord, you know we're going to have an examination tomorrow in Greek. I'm depending on you to give me the answers I need, so I'm going to bed and get a good night's sleep." Forthwith he crawled into bed and fell asleep. My father, meanwhile, burned the proverbial midnight oil and studied diligently. The next day they went to class for the examination. When the papers were returned, one of the two got a reasonably good grade and the other failed. Who, of the two, do you think failed? Without intending any irreverence it was the one who did the praying.

Why? because God never substitutes a miracle for human diligence. The Holy Spirit makes that clear to our minds.

The "devout" young man was guilty of sacrilege. It may be necessary for a student to pray that he can keep awake long enough to make adequate preparation, but the experience recounted by my father reminded me on many occasions that I should never make God responsible for accomplishing something that required my own effort.

Jesus said another function of the Holy Spirit—directed especially to those who acknowledged him as the Son of God—would be to declare to them "the things that are to come." I hardly think this implied the exercise of specific, predictive activity. Rather, the Holy Spirit refines and enriches and sensitizes our awareness of the operation of the moral law in the life of man and the universe. We then become so conscious of the inviolable operation of the law of cause and effect as to more clearly discern what is happening now and, on that basis, anticipate what will follow.

The Holy Spirit, functioning in this way, sharpening our understanding of the operation of the moral law, enables us to foresee what lies ahead. Thus, the Holy Spirit does not foster the cultivation of predictive prophetic powers so much as he enhances our appreciation of the dependable operation of the moral law so we recognize that certain causes will produce certain results involving the destiny of man.

To illustrate the point, the Holy Spirit in the best sense enabled Abraham Lincoln to foresee that a nation divided over slavery could not stand. The moral law does not favor inhumanity, however legal it may be by the laws of men. The more latitude we give for the operation of the Holy Spirit, the more helpful we are to each other.

Then Jesus had something to say about the relationship of the Holy Spirit to himself. He said, "When the Spirit of truth comes [into your life]. . . . he will glorify me, for he will take what is mine and declare it to you."

The disciples failed to grasp many qualities and characteristics of the nature and mission of Jesus while he was with them. When he was taken from them, the Holy Spirit began working through their recollections. They began to see Christ in full perspective. They proclaimed him in a more persuasive way than they ever had before. We come to a fuller appreciation of who Christ is when we permit the Holy Spirit to operate in us. So the Holy Spirit does not lead us away from Christ but into a larger recognition of him.

It is difficult to know how the Holy Spirit operates in our lives and in the world. We have about the same trouble in understanding electricity. It is available to us. It has been available to us through the centuries, but it could not be appropriated until a particular moment in history—not too long ago, at that—when it dawned on man how to channel and control it to serve human needs. A room is dark, not because electricity is not there, but because it has not been appropriated to serve that moment of darkness. Flip the switch and the room is immediately filled with light. The invisible current is summoned to work as an illuminator.

Sound waves provide a similar parallel. The atmosphere is alive with sound. But we do not hear the sounds that surround us because we are not using the instruments that can snatch these sounds out of the air so we can distinguish them. Our failure to "tune them in" does not mean they are not present.

Even so, God's Spirit is everywhere present. He is in the world. He surrounds us. But until we appropriate him by a deliberate act of invitation, he cannot fully serve us. He cannot help us as much as he would wish.

The question is not when it will please God to let electricity serve me or when it will please him to let me hear the sounds that fill the air. This is not for God to decide, but for me. Similarly, God does not delight in withholding himself from us. He eagerly awaits our appropriation of the Holy Spirit to satisfy our spiritual—even some of our temporal—needs.

Little wonder Jesus urged upon his disciples not to wait too long to receive the Holy Spirit whom he would send. "Stay in the city, until you are clothed with power from on high." How expectant Jesus was!

When they reached out to welcome the Holy Spirit, the results were overwhelming. Wonderful changes were wrought in their lives. He took his place alongside them and within them for the rest of their years on earth wherever they journeyed to serve their Lord.

"I believe in the Holy Spirit"—active in the world at large, necessary for my own well-being, and at all times holding before my finite eyes the marvel of Jesus Christ my Lord.

Prayer

Our heavenly Father, may we share this shining reality of your indwelling and continuing presence with attractive simplicity. Help us to know that this is your world and that you do not forsake it. May we see more and more of its splendor and possibility by the enlarging and constant activity of the Holy Spirit. We make this our prayer in Christ's name. Amen.

The Church Militant and Triumphant

Scripture Reading: Matthew 16:13-19; 28:19; Revelation 7:13-14

Splendor shines through the affirmation in the Apostles' Creed that proclaims: *"I believe in . . . the holy catholic Church, the communion of saints."*

Of all the phrases in the Creed, this is the one over which most Protestant Christians have halted. There are so many who seem to forget that this description of the Church was developed around A.D. 175 and that the Roman Catholic Church as a distinct and separate entity in Christendom came much later (A.D. 1054). It is likely that the Creed's description of the Church will be valid and meaningful as long as the Church on earth exists. These phrases set forth the nature and character of the Church, altogether appropriate for all Christians to use, and fully supported by scripture.

In order to explain the significance of this language of the Creed, we do well to turn to certain passages of the New Testament. First, we recall the words attributed to Jesus which appear in the Gospel according to St. Matthew. The particular passage is chapter 16, verses 13-19. This is a conversation between Jesus and the disciples whom he had separated from the multitude, taking them with him to Caesarea Philippi, a remote village about thirty-five miles north of the Sea of Galilee.

In this quiet setting Jesus talked with his dearest friends about the Kingdom of God, not only in its spiritual expression, but in its earthly manifestation as well. He began by asking them a question: "Who do men say that the son of man is?"

The responses of some of the disciples were: "Some say John the Baptist, others say Elijah." Not long before John had been beheaded on the order of Herod. Jesus was saying some of the same things John had said earlier in his wilderness preaching.

Still another answer was: "Others [think you are] Jeremiah or one of the prophets."

Then Jesus asked them directly: "Who do you say I am?" It was then that Simon Peter, the customary spokesman for the twelve, replied: "You are the Christ, the son of the living God."

Thereupon Jesus continued the conversation: " 'Simon, son of John, you are happy indeed!' answered Jesus. 'For this truth did not come to you from any human being, but it was given to you directly by my Father in heaven. And so I tell you: you are a rock, Peter, and on this rock I will build my church. Not even death will ever be able to overcome it.' " (Matt. 16:17-18. *Today's English Version*)

Of course there is an obvious play on words here, a style of speech Jesus frequently used to drive home a point. It is unfortunate that this episode should be somewhat difficult to interpret. Largely because translations from the Greek do not catch the nuances, plus the traditional interpretation put on this statement of Jesus, it has been assumed that he assigned to Simon Peter the task for creating the Church. This is the least satisfactory conclusion to draw. What is the other possibility?

Even though Jesus did not speak the Greek language, Greek is the language in which the New Testament came to us. Great care was exercised to make sure that this particular proclamation should be carefully interpreted. A distinction is deliberately and clearly made in the Greek text between the man, Simon Peter, and the confession he made: "You are the Christ." This passage can helpfully be understood in the following way without damaging the original intention of the text:

"I have called you by a symbolic name, *Petros,* so you may know that I respect you for your strength as a man. What you have said about me is true—I am Christ. So your confession that I am the Christ is really the rock on which a new fellowship for God's people will be established."

We find the right perspective in the words we sing:

> The Church's one foundation
> Is Jesus Christ her Lord;
> She is his new creation
> By water and the word.

Even the phrase "by water and the word" emphasizes the idea of the confession of who Jesus is. The water signifies baptism through which Christians make their public declaration that Jesus is Christ; and "the word" reflects the peculiar responsibility given the Church to cherish and announce the gospel which exalts Jesus as Christ.

This same passage of scripture has another statement that readily lends itself to misinterpretation. Jesus said, "I will give you the keys of the kingdom of heaven, and whatever you bind on earth shall be bound in heaven, and whatever you loose on earth shall be loosed in heaven." It is thought by some that these words were addressed to Simon Peter personally. It may be, in this instance, that they were. But we cannot afford to ignore the first resurrection statement Jesus made to all the disciples which is almost identical with what he said to Peter at Caesarea Philippi: "If you forgive the sins of any, they are forgiven; if you retain the sins of any, they are retained."

So it would seem that in making the simplest possible

interpretation of the scripture, propriety would lead us to affirm that Jesus did not select one man to become the chief architect of the Church. It is Christ alone upon whom the Church is founded. Without the acknowledgment that he is Christ there can be no Church.

The word *church* itself has important meaning. One distinguished historian, A. H. Newman, says the word *ecclesia*—from which we get the word *ecclesiastical*—denotes a calling out. He says it singularly embraces four characteristics of those who comprise the body of Christ—those who are called into this special relationship to one another and to God in Christ:

First, the entire community of the redeemed is implied by the word *ecclesia;* second, an organism that is held together by belief in a common Lord is indicated; third, participation in a common life and salvation is affirmed; and fourth, acceptance of common aims and interests is enjoined.

So the Church is a gathering together of those who are called out because of their acceptance of Jesus as Christ, who forms them into a special kind of community under his lordship.

Another fragment of scripture relates to our consideration of the significance of the Church. Again we turn to the plain words of Jesus, recorded in Matthew 28:19. Here Jesus describes the range of the mission of the Church. "Go . . . and make disciples of all nations, baptizing them in the name of the Father and of the Son and of the Holy Spirit, teaching them to observe all that I have commanded you."

The word *catholic* does not appear in the New Testament, but the universalism this word represents prevails throughout the New Testament. So when Jesus said to his friends as he commissioned them to carry forward his work, "Make disciples of all nations," he gave strong voice to the catholic spirit—the spirit of universal appeal in contrast to selectivity.

The catholic spirit is the spirit that welcomes anyone anywhere who professes faith in Jesus Christ into the fellowship of faith without regard to national origin, race, custom, language, social status, or any other differentiating condition. All a person must do to become a part of the fellowship is to make this affirmation concerning Jesus. He continues in the fellowship by observing devotedly all that Jesus taught. So all nations are embraced by the Church of Jesus Christ.

This appeal is unlike that of other religious groups of Jesus' own time. Judaism, for example, was a national religion. Jesus proposed a supranational faith capable of including all persons in all lands. The word *general* (which is synonymous with the word *catholic*) is used to designate the New Testament letters of Peter, James, John, and Jude because they were written to encourage all Christians everywhere (as unlike the Letters to the Corinthians or the one to the Ephesians). They are therefore called catholic or general epistles. Whenever a person thinks of the Church as being beyond national limitations or beyond racial exclusiveness, he is looking upon the Church as catholic. This is what it really is when it follows the admonition of Christ.

Notice, too, that Jesus obligated his followers to do more than win believers. Important as this is, it is only the first act. We might call this the function of evangelism —to persuade persons to embrace Christ as their Lord. But he commanded his disciples to fulfill another responsibility: to reach out to all persons in need. This is a mandate, not an elective.

The Church's duty and concern is not limited to those who are in face-to-face relationship. Christ expects us to reach out compassionately to persons in need wherever they are, whether we see them or not. The Church at its best is a sharing fellowship. Funds have gone out from Christian congregations in an ever-increasing flow to unfortunates around the world—feeding the hungry, clothing the naked, ministering to the sick, encouraging the impoverished, consoling the heartbroken, sheltering the ill-housed. We do this only because Christ has put in our hearts a caring spirit that we did not have before we came under his loving power. We do that which Christ wants us to do. These tasks, gladly undertaken, are one expression of the Church Militant.

When the Church Catholic becomes the Church Militant, it is the Church Missionary. How absolutely necessary it is for Christians not to lose this vision. Any encouragement we give to this missionary thrust of the faith becomes a demonstration of obedience to an expectation of our Lord. We need to ask why we do what we do in the Church.

Some years ago a member of a congregation resented a pastor who, in conscience, had to make a change in a long-established practice. Her defense was: "I don't know why you would do such a thing, after all I've done for you." He replied: "I thought all the time that everything you were doing was for Christ, and now it turns out you were only doing it for me."

I cannot imagine anything more unfortunate than for Christians to do what they do for reasons other than for Christ's sake. Do we teach a class, sing in the choir, reach out to a community need, or accept some office of responsibility in the Church merely because someone has asked us to become involved in this way? If so, is it possible that this explains the lack of exuberance in much of our "programming"? The only truly justifiable explanation for our participation in the life and work of the Church is that we do it all for Christ. Any other motivation cannot possibly add the fullest enrichment to the effort.

As a pastor I serve a congregation as my response to the mandate of my Lord. It makes me do some hard thinking sometimes to realize that he entrusts me with the care of souls. Every Christian is under the same mandate. Working side by side we are the Church Militant. We help provide Christian love to a hut village in Africa with the same concern as we reach out to ghetto captives in our hometown. We offer medical care to a leper in India as generously as we provide funds for a hospital in America. We reach out with compassion to all parts of the world where need is known as well as to those segments of our own community where need is seen.

In yet another way we are the Church Militant. When we face up to the moral implications of war, the responsibility of government to keep its honor in serving its constituency, the frightful toll of human dignity resulting from injustice, the winning of hard battles to set human priorities in focus, challenging tyranny in any form— when we engage the Church in these struggles of culture, we are the Church Militant.

The phrase "communion of saints" suggests to us that beyond believing in the Church Militant we believe also in the Church Triumphant. In the Book of Revelation, written during a time of severe persecution, John in exile on the penal island of Patmos described a vision he had of those who had already gone before him in martyrdom to be with God. He put the vision into dialogue form:

"One of the elders addressed me, saying, 'Who are these, clothed in white robes, and whence have they come?'

"And I said to him, 'Sir, you know.'

"And he said to me, 'These are they who have come out of the great tribulation; they have washed their robes and made them white in the blood of the Lamb.' "

More members of the Church are off the earth than are on it. The Church Triumphant has a larger membership than the Church Militant. We are related to it. What a marvelous privilege this is! Death cannot destroy the Church because it defies time and place.

When my father slipped away, we of the family felt there ought to be some symbolic way to signify that his whole life was given over to the service of Christ. Instead of the customary blanket of flowers spread across his casket, we placed the Christian flag. It seemed very fitting that the earthly remains of one who had served under the banner of Christ in the Church Militant should now be shrouded under that banner as he was commended into the Church Triumphant.

I do not think of those who have gone before us through the portals of death as having lost vital relationship with the Church. They are still the Church, now victorious and glorious. So we can sing:

> Yet she on earth hath union
>   With God the Three in One,
> And mystic sweet communion
>   With those whose rest is won.
> O happy ones and holy!
>   Lord, give us grace that we,
> Like them, the meek and lowly,
>   On high may dwell with thee.

A teacher of Church History has the good fortune of getting a long view. This was true of Dr. Gaius Jackson Slosser who said to his students preparing for the ministry: "I want you to always remember that you are in the Church in its infancy. There will come after you centuries hence those who will wonder what it must have been like to have lived in the twentieth century, so close to Jesus Christ!"

We need not be discouraged about the Church. True, it is forever under attack because it is forever challenging an unredeemed society. It has chronic problems of its own, for it is admittedly afflicted with many human failings. But we take heart because the Church is passing through its promising infancy, with much more sacrifice and testimony yet to be offered and put to record. So I believe in the holy catholic Church, the communion of saints.

The Church is holy, for it is of Christ, not of men. The Church is catholic, for it beckons to all men everywhere to share in its faith and fellowship. The Church is militant because it is busy with the unfinished tasks commanded by Christ. The Church is triumphant because the powers of death cannot overtake it.

This exciting affirmation has lasted through centuries, and it means as much to us today as it meant to our fathers: "I believe in . . . the holy catholic Church, the communion of saints."

Prayer

Our heavenly Father, what pleasure is added to life for those who belong to the Body of Christ! This is our highest calling, our most cherished loyalty, our most imaginative thrust of effort to meet the need of the world. As we take our places among the people of God, help us to sense that we are taking our places alongside your Son, Jesus Christ, our Lord. It is in his name we pray. Amen.

Seventh Conversation

Life's Three Greatest Anxieties Met

Scripture Reading: 1 Corinthians 15:35-50

We come now to the triumphal ending of the Apostles' Creed: *"I believe in . . . the forgiveness of sins, the resurrection of the body, and the life everlasting."* This comprises the Christian response to the three most urgent questions asked in one form or another by each succeeding generation:

1. What can be done to rid my life of its sins against God and man?
2. Will my identity outlast my life on earth?
3. When physical death overtakes me, will my life go on?

How are these anxieties dealt with by the Christian faith?

First, what can be done to rid my life of its sins against God and man? Try as we may, we find it impossible to ignore or excuse our disobedience, our ill will, our reckless temper; or to forget our harsh words and foul behavior.

The prayer in the familiar traditional Communion ritual properly reminds us that the remembrance of our misdeeds is grievous unto us. But ignoring our sins, grieving over them, minimizing them—none of these efforts to allay our distress over them is at all effective. The Apostles' Creed encourages us to explore another possibility: "I believe in . . . the *forgiveness* of sins." It is not sin in general, but sins that we must wrestle with. We need to identify them and deal with them one by one if possible.

58

A number of years ago I was absent from my pulpit, and I invited an older minister to preach in my absence. When I returned he drew me into conversation about my preaching. He was particularly troubled over the comment of a member who told him he had not heard the word *sin* in any sermon from that pulpit since I had been appointed pastor.

"That's probably true," I admitted. When I readily identified the man who made the comment, my older pastor-friend asked: "But how did you know who it was?"

"Because," I answered, "it troubles this man that I do not use the word *sin,* but I do specify in almost every sermon particular attitudes and actions that are sinful, some of which he may indulge in. His besetting sin, however, is that he gets peeved when I get specific. He would be much more comfortable if I were to preach about sin in general."

The Apostles' Creed speaks of sins, not sin. Maybe we ought to make a list of our sins and allow space to write in the way we sought or are seeking to obtain forgiveness for each offense. This would likely be for most of us a difficult but most profitable discipline.

Most of our sins are not committed directly against God, but rather against God's children. When we profane God's name or refer recklessly to the powers that belong only to him—such as invoking the word *damn* since only God really can carry out such a request—then there is direct affront to the holy. For this kind of sinning a prayer of penitence, pleading directly to God for forgiveness and a cleansing of one's tongue, is absolutely necessary if any relief is to come at all to the offender.

But our sins against one another are more frequent and, according to Jesus, must be dealt with in another way. When we considered the creedal affirmation on the "holy catholic Church," we recalled the words spoken by Jesus to the Apostles: "If you forgive the sins of any, they are forgiven; if you retain the sins of any, they are retained." When we turn to Jesus' teachings on forgiveness in the Sermon on the Mount, we find such admonitions as these:

"This is how you should pray. . . . 'Forgive us the wrong we have done, as we have forgiven those who have wronged us . . . . for if you forgive others the wrongs they have done, your heavenly Father will also forgive you; but if you do not forgive others, then the wrongs you have done will not be forgiven by your Father.' " [4]

"If, when you are bringing your gift to the altar, you suddenly remember that your brother has a grievance against you, leave your gift where it is before the altar. First go and make your peace with your brother, and only then come back and offer your gift." (Matt. 5:23-24. NEB)

"If someone sues you, come to terms promptly while you are both on your way to court; otherwise he may hand you over to the judge." (Matt. 5:25. NEB)

The clear conclusion we must draw from these and like admonitions from Jesus is that God holds us personally responsible for our human alienations. We should not pray that God will forgive us for the sins we have committed against each other, but for courage to go and seek to make amends as promptly as possible to restore the broken relationships to which we have been party. No

---

[4] From *The New English Bible.* © the Delegates of the Oxford University Press and the Syndics of the Cambridge University Press 1961, 1970. Reprinted by permission.

Christian can afford the luxury of a broken human relationship.

We believe in the forgiveness of sins—those committed against God (to be forgiven by contrite petition); those committed against each other (by offering to make right the wrong).

We are encouraged by this affirmation to move down through the years allotted us, trailing behind us as few unresolved conflicts as possible. Every unresolved relationship must be dealt with now while we have the opportunity (settled out of court, as it were) or finally adjudicated by God himself who sees deeply into our hearts.

Second, is there any provision for preserving our identity after we finish our course of life in the flesh? It is very strange that we should fear change. In the process of passing from infancy to childhood, from childhood to youth, from youth to adulthood, from adulthood to advanced age, we experience radical changes of many kinds. The lines of Henry Lyte's familiar hymn do not beg the point:

> Change and decay in all around I see;
> O thou, who changest not, abide with me.

Quite remarkably some characteristics of our nature help us maintain our identity in spite of the constantly occurring physical changes we pass through. For example, memory manages to keep past experiences intact, former friendships (sometimes with just a little prodding!), even our achievements in learning. Another intangible element in our make-up we rely on is the ability to anticipate. We are always planning ahead. We even venture to go to unfamiliar places, but our arrival there can only be confirmed by what we have heard as the testimony of others who have been there before us.

Every person is an incredible combination of the ever-changing which we can observe and the ever-changing which we experience but manage to comprehend only meagerly by exercising the five senses. We cannot feel, see, taste, hear, or smell memory. It is an intimation to us that life even now has spiritual dimension and quality. This is very helpful in developing a strong belief that we will enjoy lasting identity.

Our physical body is an appropriate temporary home for enduring personhood. Once an eighty-two-year-old woman told me she was planning to move into a better house because the one she was living in was deteriorating. She had reference to her waning physical powers, but she was not the least bit rueful. Even though our physical nature is temporary, it is sacred because it houses the spirit of a person whose identity will not be lost, a life that will never die.

It is natural for us to wonder whether or not we will continue to hold on to our identity after our physical powers cease to function and our physical body perishes. Some words from Saint Paul provide an increasingly satisfying answer to this question. *The New English Bible* renders this portion of First Corinthians like this:

Flesh and blood can never possess the kingdom of God, and the perishable cannot possess immortality. Listen! . . . This perishable being must be clothed with the imperishable, and what is mortal must be clothed with immortality. And when our mortality has been clothed with immortality, then the saying of Scripture will come true: "Death is swallowed up; victory is won!" . . . God be praised, he gives us the victory through our Lord Jesus Christ!

What a wonderful heavenly Father we have! He has provided all that is necessary to give us our identity on earth; in his providence he provides all that is necessary to give us our identity forever. So in this sense we affirm: "I believe in . . . the resurrection of the body."

Third, and closely related to this previous declaration, we have this last proclamation of the Apostles' Creed: "I believe in . . . the life everlasting." This is our Christian answer to the question: When physical death overtakes us, will our lives go on?

When Job was in dire straits, suffering terrible tortures and being made the victim of cruel sarcasm by his erstwhile friends, he cried out, "If a man die, shall he live again? (Job 14:14. KJ) The surest answer we know came from Christ, who in taking farewell of his disciples assured them: "Because I live, you will live also."

For Jesus, all men are made for immortality because God, who creates human life as an extension of his own likeness, cannot annihilate life without destroying something of himself. But our moral choices kept Jesus from giving support to an unexamined universalism. He spoke with candor about separation from God and with confidence about fellowship with God. Hell and heaven alike concerned Jesus. Whenever we read those passages in which he felt constrained to deal with questions pertaining to immortality as involving separation from God for the unrepentant—such as "a great chasm has been fixed and none may cross," ". . . the gate is wide and the way is easy that leads to destruction, and those who enter by it are many"—we get a feeling that it grieved him to say it. He knew that no life could be cast into an insensitive, unknowing oblivion. He tried by hard warning to get men to see the tragedy of rejecting their great opportunity to spend eternity in harmonious relationship with God.

The invitation he held out to those who responded to God's gracious summons was life eternal. The abundant life we enjoy by making Christ regnant in our hearts now is only a foretaste of the fuller joy that is to come. It is as if the Apostles' Creed wants to close out with the same confidence that we find in John 3:16: "God loved the world so much that he gave his only Son, that whoever believes in him should not perish but have eternal life."

So the Christian faith meets our three primary anxieties head on, enabling us to proclaim with the faithful who have gone on before us: "I believe in . . . the forgiveness of sins, in the resurrection of the body, and in the life everlasting."

Prayer

We are grateful, our heavenly Father, for a faith that gives us victory through Christ over our most difficult problems and fulfills our deepest longings. We ask of you daily courage to exercise and seek forgiveness in managing our broken human relationships. Help us honor our physical bodies as shrines temporarily housing our sacred personhood, as we anticipate at last a house not made with hands, eternal in the heavens. May we be quick to sense the brevity of our earthly sojourn as we come closer to death and become more eager for life eternal. In Christ's name we pray. Amen.